a b i d e

SURRENDER TO WIN

The reward for humility and fear of the Lord
is riches and honor and life.

- Proverbs 22:4

But now that you have been set free from sin
and have become slaves of God,
the fruit you get leads to **sanctification**
and its end, **eternal life**.

- Romans 6:22

Copyright © 2021 Shannon Guerra

With gratitude to the contributing authors, who each retain the copyright for their individual works.

All rights reserved. No part of this book may be reproduced in any form or by any electronic or mechanical means, including information storage and retrieval systems, without permission in writing from the publisher, except by reviewers, who may quote brief passages in a review.

ISBN 978-1-7360844-8-9

Published by Copperlight Wood
P.O. Box 298086
Wasilla, AK
99629

www.copperlightwood.com

Design by Shannon Guerra. Photography by Shannon Guerra, with the exception of pages 62 and 64 by Megan Ancheta.

Unless noted otherwise, scripture quotations are from the ESV® Bible (The Holy Bible, English Standard Version®), copyright © 2001 by Crossway, a publishing ministry of Good News Publishers. Used by permission. All rights reserved.

Portions of scripture in **bold** are the author's emphasis.

This title may be purchased in bulk for ministry or group study use. For more information, please email shop@copperlightwood.com.

Printed and bound in the USA.

contributors

MĒGAN ANCHETA
Kodiak kid, fearless knitter,
owner of Allergy Free Alaska, LLC
www.allergyfreealaska.com
allergyfreealaska@gmail.com

AMANDA BACON
mom of 8, lover of books and all things British, co-author of Shiny Things, co-host of All the Mom Things podcast

JESSICA DASSOW
long-time homeschool mom, chicken collector, seeker of sand & sunshine
www.planted-by-the-river.com

CYNTHIA HELLMAN
unsweetened sun tea drinker, over-analyzer with a penchant for old canning jars
www.cultivatedgraftings.blogspot.com

RENEE PETTY
lover of flowers, champion sledder, dances in the kitchen and laughs at her own jokes

contents

06
lay it down

11
dealing with the mess

16
of ducks and squirrels

19
how we thrive when the weather changes

24
it snows

26
yielding to His way

31
made to grow

35
where rest meets hospitality

36 a good plan gone sideways

39 surrendered abiding: the easiest (and hardest) way to win

44 better than the book

47 why we try

48 overtaken

53 trading ambition for trust

58 dark chocolate toffee

62 cinnamon french toast dippers

65 redeemable

71 jude 24-25

72 study guide

77 notes

lay it down

There are moms who complete their morning devotions, first cup of coffee, and kitchen chores in the early morning hours; they are already happily cooking breakfast when everyone else stumbles into the kitchen.

And then there's me. I reconciled with the guilt of not being that kind of mom a long time ago.

Nope. I'm the one who stumbles in the kitchen, often when (or after) everyone else has had breakfast. I'm the poster child for the meme that says: *Y'all go ahead and carpe diem without me, I'll catch up.*

I know it sounds super lazy, but during a long season of mothering with severe health issues, insomnia, and a baby still up at all hours of the night, I had a hard time getting anywhere before noon, even. But, hey – if you needed someone to pray for you between 2 and 6 am, I was your girl.

It seemed like a terrible time to start cutting caffeine...but there we were, thanks to those previously-mentioned health issues.

It was quite a process to figure out how to wean myself off three shots of espresso every morning when Vince had no intention of also doing so. And going cold turkey didn't seem like a good idea since I didn't want to go to prison.

This was the math conundrum: Our espresso pot makes six shots, so we would make an additional pot of decaf (yes, another six shots) so I could taper accordingly for a few days and maintain my sanity. That way I could gradually go from three shots to two, and then from two to one, and then to –

Well...um, three-quarters of a shot, and then maybe to five-eighths of a shot...

Never mind. I don't want to play anymore, this is stupid.

But after a week I was down to somewhere in the three-quarters range. It was a little fuzzy because in our attempt to keep Vin's coffee normal but reduce my caffeine intake, sometime around the midway point we confused the caff with the decaf and gave up measuring.

And now I just drink decaf. So as you can see, I survived.

I wanted coffee. But what I really wanted was a healthy body and a healthy heart, and the reward is greater than the surrender. Plus, a friend of mine texted and said, *You should feel great once you adjust, caffeine is terrible on the adrenals.*

And I texted back and said, *I think I'm already there, I'm just feeling sorry for myself.*

Because I don't know about you, but I am tired of having "just one more thing" to give up. Sugar. Bread. Sleep. Events. Expectations.

> *When Jesus had received the sour wine, he said, "It is finished," and he bowed his head and gave up his spirit.*
>
> - John 19:30

But what we see in Scripture is that when the Lord modeled surrender, the high cost came with a higher reward.

Don't mistake this – **He did not surrender anything outside of God's plan**. He did not capitulate to the money changers,[1] He didn't give in to the Pharisees,[2] and He didn't shrink from correcting His own disciples when they made well-meaning but dangerously errant remarks.[3]

Not everything we're asked to surrender is God's plan. Some things we need to continue to fight for.

But when *God* tells us to surrender something, we can count on a huge return ahead. That doesn't mean the surrender will be easy, though.

Our biggest surrenders are not over physical things, but the heart issues that we hold on to. Places we have hardened off to conviction, or desires we've turned into idols. Or, what we often see in social media lately: Personal experiences we've magnified out of proportion.

And that's a big one, because our personal experience might be all we have, but that doesn't mean it's all there is. It doesn't define an entire issue and it doesn't completely define who we are – or who others are. And when we act like it does, our experience is no longer an asset we can draw from, but a liability that expresses our immaturity. It usually shows up as pride, and reveals itself as insecurity.

In my own heart I have wrestled with questions like this: Am I bitter at this person, or do I just have good reason to not believe them? Sometimes it's hard to distinguish between bitterness/unforgiveness (which are just barely separate things themselves) and lack of trust based on past experience with certain people. And if it *is* lack of trust, doesn't that come down to needing to trust God with the situation (which sounds a lot like forgiveness, as long as boundaries are already in place) since He knows whether or not the person is really sincere or totally faking it anyway?

I think so. Partly, at least. Because ultimately, walking in forgiveness and wholeness includes surrendering all the feelings to God. When we do that, He allows us to hear His truth and then see victory we never would have achieved if we had held on to whatever it is He's asking us to lay down.

When we surrendered our oldest kid, it felt right and yet so not right. He was out on his own, going to graduate on his own, doing everything on his own. We surrendered traditional graduation events, festivities, and some dreams of what we thought things ought to look like for what they actually were. So many things. And so many times, it felt like part of me was dying.

For about a year, we didn't know if any of it worked. It was out of our hands. He was out of our hands.

But he always was, anyway. Right, parents? Just like all of our kids. Just like anything and anyone we care about. It's just such a shock to realize it sometimes.

The year passed. We waited and prayed and tried not to think too much about phone calls in the middle of the night, or other terrible possibilities.

And then, tentative steps. Signs of a wall cracking, of light breaking through. A green tendril curling out and unfurling as loosened mortar dropped to the ground and bricks started to move. And then whole sections gave way. Sunlight hit places it hadn't seen in years.

Over the following months, bricks continued to topple here and there. And finally, ten months later, we saw color where for five years there had only been blackness.

If you had asked us a year earlier, we never would have imagined the progress happening that we couldn't see. We had no idea that this kind of victory would ever be possible – much less, just twelve months later.

So my question for you is, What seems so far away now? In a year, what might that look like? Because He has breakthrough in the works that we would never expect – but He might be asking you to lay something down for it to happen.

I am praying for walls to open, to come down, to break through in hearts. For hardened areas to break in others, and in myself. Where we have hardened off to conviction, I'm praying that we will hear Him. Where we have hardened off to protect ourselves from pain, I'm praying we will be brave and willing to love again – that we will love more, in spite of pain. Because He did, for us.

dealing with the mess

A large bag of wooden clothespins showed up on my desk and a week later, it was still squatting there. And it wouldn't have been a big deal except someone opened the bag, and over the next several days the contents gradually hemorrhaged everywhere. A variety pack – dozens of clothespins, all different sizes, decorating the surface of my desk.

I love having a clean desk. But aside from moving everything to the floor (which is my normal method of cleaning it in a hurry), I have yet to figure out how to keep it that way.

On any given day, the desk is smothered under stacks of books: notebooks, school books, research books, books I'm reading. And just to be clear, when I say "stacks of books," the word stacks should be interpreted loosely. Very loosely. As in, some books truly are placed on top of each other in a (mostly) congruent, vertical direction. But others are… um…just overlapping, sort of like a giant, bloated, bookish version of Jenga.

Aside from books, there are pens, sippy cups, and other detritus constantly trafficked in and out of the office, plus the aforementioned clothespins sprinkled everywhere. It's not just my mess (you heard me mention the sippy cup, right?) but it is my mess to take care of. No one can clean it for me. Even if they wanted to, I have to do it myself. May God help them if they try; hell hath no fury like a writer-mama (or wife) who can't find the stack of books she needs to pull citations from that took her three hours to round up from all over the house in the first place.

Of course, it would help if people would stop spewing their mess in my space. I have my own junk to deal with, but we sinners share the love and we have a tendency to give each other more to forgive and clean up. We all add to each other's messes.

Oh, wait – I was talking about physical messes. Not the other kind, when we are hurting and we hurt others, and the mess goes everywhere, and it's so much harder to clean up than a hundred scattered clothespins.

May grace and peace be multiplied to you in the knowledge of God and of Jesus our Lord.
– 2 Peter 1:2

The mess the kids leave on the floor is usually theirs to clean up. But when the mess bleeds onto the desk, with all my own stuff in various states of organization and disarray, it becomes my job to take care of. Mostly, I take care of it by not allowing the mess to be made in the first place.

Boundaries, rules, whatever you call it – the desk is my space and the kids have mostly learned to respect that. Prevention is the easiest way to take care of everything, right? If we could just keep the hurtful words, the hard feelings, or the negative habits of others out of our headspace, life would be so much easier. I have my own thoughts to take captive, and that's a job of its own to deal with. But once those other things penetrate, they're my problem, too.

Oh, wait, I was talking about physical messes. I keep forgetting.

It would be easier if none of it ever happened in the first place – the physical or emotional messes – but the world is a bloody battlefield. It would be easier to just not enter the fray, but we can't prevent everything...and really, would we want to? We're made to help each other navigate the mess.

But we must be invited to do so. And if the mess is ours – whether we made it, or someone else did and now it's all over our space – we have to be the one to initiate the cleaning.

> *The LORD your God is in your midst,*
> *A victorious warrior. He will exult*
> *over you with joy, He will be quiet in*
> *His love, He will rejoice over you with*
> *shouts of joy.*
> *– Zephaniah 3:17, NASB* [4]

Most versions of this verse end with "He will rejoice over you with singing" but when I read this version and noticed the phrase "shouts of joy," the Lord told me something new.

When do parents shout for joy over their children? He asked me.

Well, I thought, parents shout for joy when they see their kids achieve – when they succeed, when they score a goal, when they win something big, when they hit a milestone. We cheer over our babies when they get their first tooth, and we whoop and holler when they take their first steps.

But as adults, all of our success, achievement, or milestones are things He does for us and through us. We know we're not doing them on our own. So why would He shout for us when He's the one doing the work?

I don't, He said. I shout for joy over you when you do something I can't do for you.

What can't You do for us? I asked.

I can't choose surrender and obedience for you, He said.

*I can't choose for you to clean up your mess. I can help you do it, but you have to want it first. I can't choose for you to stay steadfast in the battle, still fighting and standing, in spite of everything around you. I can **want** those things for you, and I can help you through them, but only you can choose to move forward in growth, instead of retreating.*

***That** is what I shout for joy over.*

> *For this very reason, make every effort to supplement your faith with virtue, and virtue with knowledge, and knowledge with self-control, and self-control with steadfastness, and steadfastness with godliness, and godliness with brotherly affection, and brotherly affection with love. For if these qualities are yours and are increasing, they keep you from being ineffective or unfruitful in the knowledge of our Lord Jesus Christ.*
>
> *– 2 Peter 1:5-8*

Just as the main battle we fight is less about violent movement and more about steady abiding, the victories He shouts over in our lives are the small-but-huge efforts that come in the quiet:

- When we choose truth over rumor, or grace and forgiveness over hard feelings.
- When we address our own bad habits, and choose healthier thought patterns.
- When we choose to pray and thank God even when things look ugly.
- When we tackle the hard-but-necessary conversation when it seems easier to let it slide and pay the consequences later.
- When we push forward in doing the good things: Gratitude, repentance, teachability, honor.
- When we stop to hug the kid, kiss the spouse, and clean up our mess…even if someone else started it.

He can't wait for us to take those first steps, and to cheer us on as we keep moving forward. It's our obedience, integrity, and gritty steadfastness that He shouts over.

# of ducks and squirrels

BY RENEE PETTY

I read a meme once that made me literally laugh out loud: *I don't have ducks. I don't have a row. I have squirrels and they're drunk.* My dad used to always tell me I needed to "get my ducks in a row," and despite all honest attempts, drunk squirrels more accurately describe what I usually ended up with. On a good day, maybe they were in a row, but not likely. I think, if we are being real with one another, most of us have nothing close to resembling nice rows of ducks moving happily along, all according to plan. Even if we do, all it takes is one hawk out of nowhere to send them scattering.

This is life, ducks and squirrels, rows and chaos. If there is one lesson 2020 should have taught us it is that real control is either an illusion or frustratingly temporary. It is the desire to micromanage and sort our lives that is often the cause of our biggest stumbling blocks in relationship with Jesus. We want to trust, but we would prefer to know the outcomes of all things before we fully surrender our will to His. If we can have our ducks, we are good, but if there's a hint of disorder or uncertainty, we wrest our lives back from Him. Most of us spend the bulk of our days in this back and forth. It's an exhausting, defeating way to live (have you ever seen a drunk squirrel?), and Jesus came to show us a better way.

Then Jesus told his disciples, "If anyone would come after me, let him deny himself and take up his cross and follow me. For whoever would save his life will lose it, but whoever loses his life for my sake will find it.
- Matthew 16:24-25

Whoever loses His life for my sake will find it... when we lose our lives to Jesus, we find what we were looking for. When we choose to release control, to let go of our desire to micro-manage all those ducks, He meets us there. We think we are giving everything up, but really, we are finding it all. Our attempts to control are feeble and futile; surrendering to His Sovereignty brings rest.

Surrender is simple, but not easy, and it is the one thing you can control. He who created all things, and knows all things, has a purpose and a calling for your life. What you see as chaos and uncertainty, He sees as His plan for your good and His glory. Friend, forget about your ducks being perfectly aligned, or rounding up all the inebriated squirrels in your life. Whenever you are tempted to sort the chaos, when it looks like drunk animals are reigning, remember there is One greater, and He is working in it all.

how we thrive when the weather changes

I plowed through half a bar of dark chocolate, desperately trying to make good choices when the kitchen was full of caramel corn, chocolate truffles, cookies, and other incendiary devices.

I needed wisdom for a snowy school day, when the dishes and laundry and assignments were overflowing, the sound of kids raking through Legos was overwhelming, and the baby was outgrowing his clothes as fast as the weather was changing. Time is a capricious servant that moves fast or slow at whim, and is only mastered by His continual presence.

> *Seek the Lord and his strength;*
>   *seek his presence continually!*
> – Psalm 105:4

In a season of wondering, wandering, and questioning our direction, we have to consider this: There's a time to be still, and a time to move. But sometimes we use "being still" as an excuse *not to move.* If God has already given us a direction, but we don't like it and we're, ahem, "waiting for confirmation," that's not being still; that's disobedience. God can't move us forward when we're holding back. A ship at anchor cannot be steered.

But also, there's this: If a significant situation has recently come to an end (like a relationship, a responsibility, or a season of life), we may be averse to the stillness that comes after it. If waiting in a transition period is too uncomfortable, we may see everything as a sign to move forward in order to resist the stillness He's calling us to.

If something has recently come to an end, we need to have stillness to process correctly. We need time to come out of the fog so we can see clearly. We need to heal well. If we avoid those things out of restlessness, we'll move into the next season without the full wholeness we're meant to walk in. But when we wait, process, and heal in the stillness, and then move forward when He tells us, we're positioned for great joy and victory. That's the sweet spot.

I have learned as a mom, wife, friend, student, writer, or any other role I'm in at any given time, that my role requires Jesus. It requires prayer in the inconvenient and unholy moments; I require His presence in the mundane and the mess. I have to give Him the scary things and let go of my stubbornness in order to move where He wants me to go.

If I want to thrive (and I do!) I have to settle for the best – which is always His best. Because my best, if it's different from His best, will always fall short.

Often enough, when we think we are protecting ourselves, we are struggling against our rescuer.
– Marilynne Robinson [5]

A few years ago I got my first spider plant, and it erupted into dozens of little spider plant babies that needed trimmed from it. I was so excited; dozens of new little plants to scatter all over the house and give away to friends.

So I tried — twice — to get them to root, and they all died each time. It felt like such a waste.

It took almost two years for that many baby plants to grow from it again. As I watched them shoot out of the big plant, I was at a loss and didn't know what to do. So mostly, I did nothing, except give some of the baby shoots to friends. Surely they would know what to do. Because I didn't. I had tried, and failed, and tried and failed again.

I must be okay at taking care of this spider plant, but going to the next level must not be for me. I'd just leave that for others.

But then...I tried one more time. I'm a stubborn beast and had the entire internet in my tool chest.

So I tried a different technique – the one I had refused to try before, because I thought the way I was doing it was easier, cleaner, and more likely to work...even though it failed both times. (You can see how our stubbornness often equals stupidity.)

And, LO AND BEHOLD: Suddenly I was the happy owner of EIGHT new spider plants. Go big or go home.

Our hearts have to grow in courage (read: surrender) before our tent pegs can be stretched wider, yes?

Could it be that when we are most tempted to wash our hands of something (or someone) that that is when we are actually closest to seeing breakthrough?

We have to need Him to hear Him. We have to move out of our comfort zone to need Him. And we have to trust Him in surrender before we can start that process. But once we surrender and move out of His way, He shines through us.

So friends, a word for those of us who need it:

Failing doesn't mean we're failures.

It doesn't mean the door is closed.

It doesn't mean the dream is dead and better left for others to live out.

It means we need to keep trying, and go a different direction.

Try it a different way. Do it the way you refused to do it before.

There's life just waiting to take root and thrive when we do.

"It snows!" cries the Traveler, "Ho!" and the word
 Has quickened his steed's lagging pace;
The wind rushes by, but its howl is unheard,
Unfelt the sharp drift in his face;
For bright through the tempest his own home appeared,
Ay, though leagues intervened, he can see:
There's the clear, glowing hearth, and the table prepared,
And his wife with her babes at her knee;
Blest thought! How it lightens the grief-laden hour,
That those we love dearest are safe from its power!

- Sarah Josepha Hale [6]

yielding to His way

BY JESSICA DASSOW

We relaxed on the couch, content and bone-tired after such a full day of family fun, when he plopped down on the ottoman by our feet. His obvious resolve and the nature of his calm smile revealed right away that we were about to hear something important. I took a deep breath and held it. Without wasting any time, he put it out there, his eyes communicating concerned love for his mother and desire for his parents to truly hear what he had to say: He was enlisting in the Marines.

We sat still, barely breathing, listening hard to hear the why and to understand while a million thoughts swirled through my mind of an unexpected and uncertain future – pictures I didn't want to see and legitimate fears intermingled with pride and such deep love for this handsome young man. I wanted to tangibly encourage and support – oh how I wanted to! But no words could come to express that; only two tears sliding one by one – my emotions leaking, despite my wish to keep them inside.

Several days went on and I battled fear and anxiety as I tried to wrap my mind around this new thing God was calling me to as a mom who would send her son to serve our country. I wanted to focus on the goodness and the adventure, but instead I wrestled to cast out images of thirteen U.S. Servicemen who just days before, returned to their mothers in flag-covered caskets. You see, sometimes my emotions and body refuse to line up with my mind.

My mind knows the truth, and I believe it – God's plans for me and my family are for our good and for His own glory:

> *And we know that for those who love God, all things work together for good, for those who are called according to his purpose.*
> *– Romans 8:28*

But my emotions can run pell-mell and my body dump cortisol like a dump truck at times as I struggle to rein them in.

Perhaps you too have a situation that has your emotions wrapped around the axle? Let's remember together that He is 100% in control, He isn't surprised or caught off-guard. His plans cannot be thwarted, and none of us will live one day less or one day more than He has ordained from the foundation of the earth.

> *Your eyes saw my unformed substance; in your book were written, every one of them; the days that were formed for me, when as yet there was none of them.*
> *– Psalm 139:16*

As His people, we have a job to do on this earth – works to partake in which He has established – to make disciples, to be salt and light, to seek justice, and to love kindness.

> *He has told you, O man, what is good; and what does the Lord require of you but to do justice, and to love kindness, and to walk humbly with your God?*
> *– Micah 6:8*

This will look any number of ways, and we each must do what He calls us to do. Furthermore, because He is with us, we can step forward victoriously into our calling with courage.

> *I have said these things to you, that in me you may have peace. In the world you will have tribulation. But take heart; I have overcome the world.*
> – John 16:33

We know these things for certain. So how do we restrain our emotions when life throws us for a loop? How do we calm our fears?

Fear is not from the Lord, and it needs to be cast out. Sometimes my emotions and body just seem to do their own thing, and I feel powerless to rein them in despite confessing all this truth and even more truth – loudly and vehemently at times: Fear! Do you hear me? Go back to the fiery pit you came from, because you have no place in my life!

> *For God gave us a spirit not of fear but of power and love, and of self-control.*
> – 1 Timothy 1:7

Confessing truth at every turn during the days following my son's announcement, yet recognizing the enemy of my soul was still having a heyday firing his flaming arrows, I asked close friends to pray alongside me. I needed help to kick the fear and uncertainty to the curb and get my emotions and cortisol dumps in line with what my mind knew and believed to be true according to God's Word.

We need each other in this war, sisters and brothers in Christ. We can't do it alone, and we're not meant to. There's such power in sitting at God's feet with and for one another.

The overwhelming clanging of thoughts and images in my mind began to clear. I felt the first pings of peace being received deeply into my soul.

God recalled to my mind a younger mom who, when a knock came to the door, invited a meth addict in to warm up for a few minutes. She made the woman tea and shared Jesus with her. That mom had no fear because she knew God called her to it. She didn't think twice, she just did it because it was her obvious assignment. When she discovered the addict stole stuff, that mom led her children to have compassion on the addict and pray for her.

God reminded me of how He directed that same young mom to bake cookies and take them, kicking beer cans away from the door, to the drug-dealing, thieving neighbors. She didn't think twice, just took the assignment. She took her young children along so they could learn and practice radical love. And God reminded me of what He did in the hearts of those neighbors as a result of that small act of obedience. The children also saw, and they learned, too.

As I thought of those long ago memories, I realized I'm still that same mom who can obediently surrender to the mission at hand. Although I'm older and somewhat wiser, at times I get a bit too comfortable in formulating how I'd like life to be. Sometimes I think twice. Sometimes I don't think at all. By God's grace and through His power I will walk out the works He sets before me in these days and in this season with that same courage. I will rejoice and not fear when my children begin to take their own steps of faith and obedience.

Surrender. I needed to surrender to His plan of me becoming a military mom. I needed to stop contemplating that life was taking a different direction than what I expected and planned, and instead seize hold of the task and adventure before me. I needed to quit entertaining the lies my enemy was hurling at me and cast out the images he viciously placed in my mind. I would let the truth of God's sovereignty over our lives root deeply in as I let go. With His help, I would walk God's calling in obedience, no matter the cost.

The stakes are too high to cower, or to be paralyzed by fear, or to be bewildered over the unknowns. So, friend, whatever that thing is that's caught you by surprise? Give it up. Surrender it completely to the Lord. Fighting against God's will in your life equals exhaustion and anxiety. But if you are His, you have peace and freedom and victory, if only you'll surrender!

He's asking us to grab His hand and rise victoriously to a new level, to be at peace and to thrive in our calling, come what may, knowing it is for our good and for His glory. He promises to be with us – to lead us every step of the way. Bravely receive His peace and embrace the stretching of this new season. This is an opportunity to grow in faith and trust of our Lord.

made to grow

There are seasons of motherhood when I spend all day saying stupid things like "No, you may not swing the cat in the pillowcase," and "No, you may not take the cat outside on a leash," and "No, you may not put the baby overalls on the cat," and also (lest you think every wild idea around here involves a cat) "Why are you on that part of our roof?" By the time we make it to bedtime, our sons think putting pajamas on is a contact sport and I am so sick of refereeing the game that I want to eject everyone from it.

And that's just normal parenting. Throw in special needs or health issues or a major home repair, and everything feels overwhelming and out of proportion. Life is hard, full of real problems that platitudes have no answers for. In those seasons, we dread the morning and the new day. We do not know what the future holds, but if past performance is any indicator of future results, it seems safer to just stay in bed.

Some of my kids have special needs, and usually those needs are far more behavioral than physical. Sometimes they just refuse to grow and move forward, and there is nothing I can do to move them past the place they've dug their heels in.

And the thing I have learned — and am still learning — is that parenting, adoption, and special needs are not necessarily pass/fail endeavors. Because the child makes his or her own choices, and eventually the child has to learn to clean up their own mess. We all do, right?

We're all meant to grow. And the more a child refuses to grow, the more God grows me. Either way, God brings healing and wholeness. It's just more fun when we don't resist it.

If God is giving you the opportunity to grow and heal in these days, to rip something out and start over again, then for the love of all that is holy, do not squander it. Do not shy from the Lord's probing questions, gentle correction, or nudges toward alignment and surrender. Our joy is at stake in these opportunities to clean up the mess.

We have to do the heart-work of wholeness and forgiveness, of understanding our triggers, of maturing past that old, unattractive hang up, whatever it is. The healing can come in just a few minutes or it can take years, but the timeline rests on our own willingness to surrender.

Here's a good word for us: The sun doesn't insist on shining on everything all the time; it surrenders every day. It yields to clouds and isn't diminished by the presence of something that blocks its light. It's not in competition with any other light or any other thing that gets in its way and creates a shadow. It just keeps shining, doing what it was made to do.

Every night, it is beautiful in surrender. And regardless of how cold or cloudy it was the day before, it never fails to rise the next day. That might be a word for us, too.

Sooner or later things start to take shape and we can see what the Maker is up to. And it's always good...eventually.

But surrender is hard. Haaaaarrrd, say it with me in four syllables. If it wasn't, would it be surrender at all? But it is also powerful, because surrender is also birthing, bringing new life. And when we see the fruit on the other side of it, we see the beauty and joy and breakthrough that come from laying down our agenda for His.

It doesn't matter if it's homeschooling, writing a book, parenting, learning anything new, or finally mastering the act of getting dressed in the morning without tangling up your pantleg and tripping yourself (hey, I only write about what I know), we are always learning and growing.

Or, we ought to be. There are those who choose to stagnate, but that's probably not you.

So, a word of encouragement: If you are feeling the burn of an uphill climb, it's because you're going somewhere. Stretching. Moving. Making strides. Gaining ground. Advancing. Moving forward. Going places.

Once you surrender, the unexpected won't stop you. Mistakes, once realized, confessed and yielded to God, will only advance you further.

So, press in – there is no setback God won't use to move you forward when you walk in surrender to Him.

Rest meets hospitality when we value people over presentation.

a good plan gone sideways

BY AMANDA BACON

The morning totally bombed. It was the first day of a much-needed break from our normal routine and I was looking forward to beginning a vacation of fun, intentionality and relaxation. We all needed it.

We'd spent the year living in the middle of a whole-house remodel with kids displaced in rooms that weren't bedrooms while using cardboard boxes as dressers. Our whole life had been stored in the shed in the backyard, and the remodel had taken every ounce of time and energy in addition to still working on our marriage, jobs, school, parenting, and feeding everyone.

When that first official day of vacation came, my expectations were running high. Hope was thick, but so was my lingering edginess and the deep burden I'd been carrying around.

We had plans we'd been looking forward to that first morning, but everything fell apart in the most frustrating way. A million things went wrong and I had to fight back the tears.

For starters, our 12-passenger van only had enough seats to hold six of the nine of us who were trying to leave for an appointment. The seats had been removed the day before so we could use the van to haul something, but unfortunately our morning outing wasn't factored in and the seats weren't re-installed. We didn't realize this until we went to the driveway to load up with just enough time to make it without being late.

Then, as we tried to hurriedly install enough seats for us to leave, we realized someone had tied two of the booster seats together in an impossible knot while playing around the day before and we needed to separate them in different rows as we pieced the van seats back together.

At this, along with the frustration toward the young knot-tying expert that kept getting into scrapes, I exclaimed, "I give up. We're not going. It's just not working."

I stomped inside and collapsed alongside my bed. I thought, Why is everything so hard? Why can't just one thing I try to do feel fun and easy?

As I knelt by my bed looking like some Precious Moments figurine, I did not feel one bit precious. I felt like Macho Man Randy Savage and I seriously wanted to snap into someone.

It wasn't my kids' fault.
It wasn't my fault.
It wasn't anyone's fault.
It *just was.*

It was a moment that could be redeemed, or it was a moment I could have stayed mad and bitter about. I could have let all the frustrations and hardship of the year sit with me in that moment, or I could see it for what it was: a bump in the road of normal life.

It took a few minutes, but then I remembered Who lives in me.

I stopped stewing and asked God to help me see what was true.

I texted my husband and a couple friends, asking them to pray for me.

Then I sat up and made a decision to not let this setback set me back.

We redeemed the day and made the best of it. We missed our morning outing, but I was able to reschedule it.

Maybe today totally bombed for you too. Can we let these types of setbacks be a mere bump in the road of normal life without letting all of life's frustrations taint it?

We will be okay.

Repeat after me:

God is with me and will never fail me. This setback does not have to set me back. I will breathe and show my family how to handle normal bumps in the road. I will not blow it out of proportion. If I need to apologize and make things right, I will. May I never forget that trials produce the kind of character God is looking for in me.

I'd love for the rest of my hard days to look more Precious Moments than Macho Man, but if not, I know God will walk with me, and that's more than enough for me.

surrendered abiding: the easiest (and hardest) way to win

During a big, weird season of highs and lows, we needed to make some decisions – adulting is fun like that, yes? – and during my Bible reading I was in the middle of both Jeremiah and Hebrews. They were pulling at me like two ropes at different angles, keeping me upright.

In Jeremiah, there's a king named Zedekiah who had no mind of his own; as you read his story, you see this theme of him being persuaded by others constantly. Instead of walking in the authority he had, he is constantly directed by the advice of others (some good, some bad) and he could've saved himself a lot of trouble if he had bothered to talk to the Lord and hear Him for himself.

But, well…he didn't.

Let's run through a quick condensed version of his story. Warning: These are all *extremely* rough paraphrases. Ready? Three chapters in ninety seconds, go!

To open the scene, Jeremiah is accused of deserting and sent to prison. King Zedekiah goes to him in secret and asks for a word from the Lord. Jeremiah says, "You're about to be overrun by the King of Babylon – and by the way, why the heck am I in here? Do something about it or I will die." And Zedekiah, to his credit, sent him to a safer place.[7]

But then some other people told Zedekiah what to do – and these guys were not in the practice of hearing from the Lord. Nope, they were angry at Jeremiah for warning them about the impending attack, which was a prophecy they didn't want to hear. He told them that if they fight, they will die, but **if they surrender, they will live**. So these guys told Zedekiah that Jeremiah should be put to death, and the King With No Mind of His Own said, "Okay, sure, that sounds like a great idea," and they threw him into a cistern.[8]

Fortunately, a good guy named Ebed-melech (which surprisingly never topped the lists of popular baby names) intervened for Jeremiah. How do you think he did that? He tells the king what to do, of course: "Hey King, that was stupid – those guys are evil. Jeremiah's going to die if you leave him there."

The king, presumably after scratching his armpit, says, "Uh...okay, take some men and go save him." So he does that,[9] and ancient Google databases show a slight bump in babies named Ebed-melech around 600 B.C.

Then Zedekiah sends for Jeremiah again and asks him to divulge all he knows. Jeremiah answers, "Dude, what kind of an idiot do you think I am? You'll have me put to death, and you never listen to me anyway."

The king assures him that he would never do such a thing. So Jeremiah lays it out there again. **"The Lord says you have to surrender or die. There's no escape.** So sorry."

The king says he's afraid of being treated cruelly if he surrenders. Jeremiah says, "No worries! Obey, and it will be well for you. But if you disobey, you'll regret it. All your fears and more will come to pass."[10]

I bet you know what happened. The King With No Mind of His Own followed his fears[11] instead of the Word of the Lord. And it did not go well with him.

Zedekiah didn't listen to the prophet of God, and instead of surrendering, he ran with fear – and fear overcame him. He obeyed what his eyes could see, and he lost his eyes. But before he lost his eyes, his sons were slaughtered in front of him.

He lost everything. But his fears only came to pass because he ran with them.

The nature of surrender is that it's always the thing we're resisting, and it's often the thing we are dreading. We only surrender to God – not to fear, not to pressure, not to the idols of our own making. But the things we surrender to Him are usually our own fears, pressures, and idols.

And what's trickier about surrender is that sometimes we are supposed to fight. Sometimes when everything looks like it's over, we're supposed to stand, steadfast.

How do we know the difference? Only by abiding. It's the easiest, and the hardest, and the only way to know.

> *Therefore take up the whole armor of God, that you may be able to withstand in the evil day, and having done all, to stand firm.*
> *- Ephesians 6:13*

Could it be that abiding is the battle?

Zedekiah could have fought that battle, but he didn't. He could have abided for himself instead of relying on others to do the listening and leading for him. At the very least, he could've listened to the counsel of those who *were* abiding, since he wasn't. But he didn't do that, either.

God's promise was real. The promise was there for him, for his good, for his taking – but he had to trust God to get it. He had to know that God was good; that God had good things for him, and would take care of him. But he didn't.

Instead, he went with what his eyes could see, and his eyes failed him.

And I see the parallel so clearly in our lives – and we, too, have a choice to make. **We also have to choose to trust what the Lord has said over what we see.** And what He has said and is still saying is, *Your breakthrough is coming. It's already here, you just don't see it yet. And more is still coming. Hold on and be faithful. Just keep doing the task at hand.*

Stand. Surrender. Be steadfast, and trust Me.

The cost of obedience is never as high as the cost of following fear. Had Zedekiah followed the promise that he couldn't see, they all would've been saved. When the word of the Lord is clear, there is so much at stake in our obedience.

But I told you, I was also reading in Hebrews. And the juxtaposition of those two sections made it obvious that God was in charge of the curriculum. So there was also this regarding perseverance in the face of fear and attack:

> *Therefore, since we are surrounded by so great a cloud of witnesses,* **let us also lay aside every weight** *–*

Let me interrupt here to point out that **fear is a weight that we tend to carry**, yes?

> *...and* **sin which clings so closely**, *and* **let us run with endurance the race that is set before us**, *looking to Jesus, the founder and perfecter of our faith, who for the joy that was set before him endured the cross, despising the shame, and is seated at the right hand of the throne of God.*
>
> **Consider him who endured from sinners such hostility against himself**, *so that you may not grow weary or fainthearted.*
>
> *- Hebrews 12:1-3*

And also here, regarding obedience:

> For the moment **all discipline seems painful rather than pleasant** –

(Sounds like surrender, yes?)

> ...but later it yields the peaceful fruit of righteousness to those who have been trained by it.
>
> Therefore lift your drooping hands and strengthen your weak knees, and make straight paths for your feet, so that what is lame may not be put out of joint but rather be healed.
>
> - Hebrews 12:11-13

So we can stand. Having fought the battle by abiding, hearing, obeying, waiting, and trusting, we stand in surrender for whatever He has for us.

We can trust that it is good – beyond good – no matter what our eyes see. Because that's who He is, and He can't help but be good to us when we stop fighting Him.

better than the book

BY CYNTHIA HELLMAN

I listened to the stories from my daughter's mouth but didn't heed the voice of the Holy Spirit. Instead, I eyed the book she was gushing about and smiled, feigning interest. Every time she brought it up, I resisted internally, but I hadn't sat down with Jesus and talked it through. There was *something* niggling in the periphery, but I hadn't taken the time to bring it into focus and meditate on what God was trying to get through my thick skull.

This is a theme with me. It's a good thing God loves me, because most days I prove just how dense a human being can be. Anyone relate?

There's something skeptical about surrendering in order to win. After all, gain isn't found in giving up, right? From the time we are young, we are taught to finish and finish well. Finish your veggies to enjoy dessert. Finish the book series to have closure and satisfaction. Finish studying to ace the test. Finish the internship to land the envied salary. Finish the vows to celebrate your golden anniversary.

Where does surrender play into this?

In this world, surrender is weakness. Surrender is nothing more than waving the white flag of shame. Surrender is quitting, and quitting is for losers who don't want trophies and dessert.

What makes sense to the world is topsy-turvy from God's blueprint. He has a reputation for using the simple to confound the learned. He upsets the applecart. Often. He chooses the second-born, the lame, the slow of tongue, the sinner. The Pharisees hear gibberish. Those who have ears to hear can hear the sweet voice of their Savior. None of it makes sense on the surface, but God is always moving, always speaking. And a common refrain heard is one of surrender.

I began to feel downright belligerent every time the book was mentioned, and all of it came to a head when a message from it was brought into sharp clarity. Oh. **That's** *what you were trying to tell me, wasn't it, Lord?* Time to repent, pray with a tearful girl, talk through subtle wiles of the Enemy, repent some more, and remove the offending book.

The lesser had to be surrendered in order for the Greater to be embraced. If surrendering to win seems paradoxical, it's time to adjust our sight. If our eyes consume the worries of this world, focusing on the waves crashing underfoot, we will sink. Every time. When we set our eyes on the high places and choose to surrender, the conundrum is shattered with a stone of remembrance. May we erect an altar of surrender!

Oh friends, surrender is the sweetest mourning. There is a momentary grief for what is placed on the altar. Our limited vision sees the temporal, but the alternative to surrendering is nothing short of death. The Enemy would have us white-knuckle the rails lining the wide way to utter destruction.

We surrender all that is *less than* when we press on toward a goal we can't always clearly define, but that we know is good because He is good. Sometimes, obedience is hard won. Those are the sweetest victories.

As we snuggled together, I saw the tear tracks still on her cheeks from our difficult conversation. It's never easy to surrender; if it were, it would be pointless. Despite the allure of finishing the book series, she chose surrender. Since then, a weight has been lifted, a foothold demolished. What had become clouded became crystal-clear, with impurities engulfed in the Refiner's fire.

Surrendering in order to be victorious is a terrible military strategy, but it's a powerful weapon in the hands of a believer. And *that*, my friends, is better than any book series.

You must ask for God's help.

Even when you have done so,
it may seem to you for a long time
that no help, or less help than you
need, is being given. Never mind.
After each failure, ask forgiveness,
pick yourself up, and try again.

Very often what God first helps us
toward is not the virtue itself
but just this power of always
trying again. [12]

In one sense, the road back to God is a road of moral effort, of trying harder and harder. But in another sense it is not trying that is ever going to bring us home. All this trying leads up to the vital moment at which you turn to God and say, "You must do this. I can't." [13]

— C.S. Lewis

overtaken

The old journal entry was flagged with a yellow sticky note, dated from July of 2017, and it started with this verse:

And all these blessings shall come upon you and overtake you, if you obey the voice of the Lord your God.
- Deuteronomy 28:2

Overtake. As in, catch up to you from behind, and go ahead of you. Those things you've striven for without seeing fruit – those blessings will catch up and go farther than you expect when you are faithful to obey.

I just laid Finn down for his nap, pulling the door shut behind me so the light wouldn't wake him up. I watched his fluffy blond head disappear in the darkness and I covered him with his blanket.

And I knew he was there though I couldn't see him.

I touched his forehead in the blackness and he was just as real as when the door was open and the light spilled in.

And God said, *Those things you can't see, that fruit you've been praying for, is just as real as Finnegan. The healing for your kids. The healing in your hearts. The writing career, the new home with space for kids who need it, having Vince home and doing work and ministry together – it's just as real, even though you haven't seen it yet. It's just as real as this baby sleeping in his dark room. You can touch him and prove to yourself that what your eyes can't see is still real.*

Keep praying for what you can't see, He said. *Soon the light will come on and you'll be amazed with what's been there all along, waiting to emerge with vivid color and beauty.*

And we *have* seen it – or, most of it, at least. Eight months after I wrote that, we found out Vince could quit his job so we could do the thing we had prayed about for years but never really believed was possible: write full time from home.

So we spent weeks preparing and planning, and my husband turned in his resignation. We were ready. We were doing this. We were nervous, but excited.

And then ten days later, we found out we were pregnant. No insurance, no benefits. And no going back.

> *The manna ceased. Stopped. All done, finis. There was no going back, no back-up plan –*
> *the water was rushing in the Jordan River behind them, and in front of them was a fortified*
> *city to conquer. In between, they were all in.* [14]

And this is where we have lived ever since: Learning publishing, distribution, formatting, cover design, even blankety-blank page numbers. Doing the homeschooling, ministry, home repairs, research, the whole shebang, all the stuff, any seventy hours of the week we want. We are living the dream, but the dream is a ton of work.

We have swung up and down the spectrum of, "Oh, God, how can we do this?" to "Oh my word, I think it's working!" and back again to "I have no idea what to do, and I hate this part." Internet tutorials were made for such a time as this.

> *Maybe if the manna had kept coming, some of them might have thought to go back to the river,*
> *hoping that God would hold back the water again and let them return.* **But no, this was a sharp**
> **knife, cutting off any hesitation to obey** *– no manna meant they were invested, they were staying,*
> *and the only direction they were going was forward.*
>
> *And my life needs this. A commitment I need to let go of, an unhealthy relationship that needs*
> *firm boundaries, that threshold I need to walk through:* **I've been using the blunt edge of a knife**
> **to whack at them every once in a while, but those things have been on the cutting board for a**
> **long time.** *Probably way too long, and we're not getting anywhere.*
>
> **Turn it over**, *He tells me. And I squirm a little about it, but He's right there, saying, Don't hesitate*
> *to obey, Love. You are invested, you are staying, the only direction you're going is forward.* [15]

But before we were able to turn it over full time, we turned it over in increments, whenever Vince could take an extra week or two off work so we could make some progress forward. It was practice and preparation. We were investing time, effort, and money into something that we didn't know for sure would ever see fruition.

The comfortable, familiar routines (and paychecks) were hard to let go of, though.

He told me He had something wonderful for me if I would just hold out my hands and accept it. The problem was I was already holding onto something else, and I didn't want to let go.

And He was patient with me – because He is like that – and He said, Whenever you're ready for it, Love. But how long do you really want to wait for Me to bless you with this?

I realized I was being an idiot and stopped dragging my feet. I let go, grabbed hold, and hung on. [16]

Five months later (and seven months pregnant), we each published a book that had spent years on the back burner, and we saw glimpses of healing and growth in our kids who desperately needed it. It didn't look like what we dreamed of, or even what we planned for. And no, it has never looked opulent or magazine-perfect. But it looks like He's had His hand upon us in ways that we never realized.

⁴And Gideon came to the Jordan and crossed over, he and the 300 men who were with him, exhausted yet pursuing. ⁵ So he said to the men of Succoth, "Please give loaves of bread to the people who follow me, for they are exhausted, and I am pursuing after Zebah and Zalmunna, the kings of Midian." ⁶And the officials of Succoth said, "Are the hands of Zebah and Zalmunna already in your hand, that we

It looks like the threshold He asked us about several years ago.

I've learned since then that letting go happens in phases. He was preparing us then for what He offered later – and the letting go we did then was the sharp knife preparing us for what was ahead.

> He said to them, "It is not for you to know times or seasons that the Father has fixed by his own authority. But you will receive power when the Holy Spirit has come upon you, and you will be my witnesses in Jerusalem and in all Judea and Samaria, and to the end of the earth."
> – Acts 1:7-8

I have so badly wanted to know the times and seasons, but I am learning to win through surrender. There's nothing wrong with planning or preparing when it's anchored in surrender, but He's teaching me that if given the choice between knowing the plan or having the power,[17] I want power every time.

And that's nothing to be ashamed of or shy about, because when we choose surrender over control, it's what He wants for us, too.

trading ambition for trust

My husband read to the littles during the day, and he read to them again that night because I was too exhausted and out of breath.

I could hear him upstairs getting them all to bed – directing traffic, sending some kids to the bathroom to go potty, and praying with others. I was downstairs on the couch, doing nothing but working through braxton-hicks contractions. This was during that last pregnancy I told you about earlier – we had no insurance, and no income that we didn't create for ourselves. I was becoming less and less able to do the things that needed to be done, and I am a doer who *loves* to get all the things done. It was an incredibly helpless feeling.

It was a season of learning, resting, and trusting more than doing. I felt the stretching, and the stretching didn't feel very worthwhile. My brain was like, HEY! *We need to be productive! We've got things to do, and this stretching and learning and trying and failing and redoing things isn't getting them done!*

But then the Lord told me, *This stretching **is** the production, Love.*

Oh.

He said, *This is where I bear fruit in you, as My image bearer. Doing hard things. Learning new things. Staying humble in the growing process, stretching past your confidence and comfort zone. This is where I make You more like me.*

Ohhh.

So I was right there, getting ready to hit midweek with my ambitious to do list still looking very unfinished, learning to let Him reconcile what He wanted to do in me with what I wanted to do on that list. And as I exchanged striving for surrender, He was bringing them into alignment.

Part of this meant that I had to learn to yield to the Sabbath. I had never worked Monday through Friday before, and the Lord had to boss me a little about it:

Take at least one day off. Rest. Use it.

Do not, I repeat, do not plow through both days only to arrive at Monday and do it all over again for another five days. Or fifty days.

Even if you feel behind, you can end the week strong. How? Surrender: Give the overwhelm to Me. Trust Me with what you cannot do. Less than that is idolatry, worshipping yourself.

Ouch. Yeah.

> *Blessed is the man who trusts in the Lord,*
>   *whose trust is the Lord.*
> *He is like a tree planted by water,*
>   *that sends out its roots by the stream,*
> *and does not fear when heat comes,*
>   *for its leaves remain green,*
> *and is not anxious in the year of drought,*
>   *for it does not cease to bear fruit.*
>
> *- Jeremiah 17:7-8*

When we feel hemmed in, restless, and too small to leap the barrier, it might be that the obstacle blocking our progress is actually the river God has planted us next to in order to provide for us in a dry season.

Our productivity isn't always about what we can accomplish. Neglecting the Sabbath to get more work done is like neglecting to tithe so you can make more money. A short-term fix might feel good, but in the long term you've sacrificed God's hand of protection and blessing. Bad move. He promises to bless those who trust Him, and He is faithful. The Bible is full of those promises. (It also says a few things about idolatry.)

See that you do not refuse him who is speaking. For if they did not escape when they refused him who warned them on earth, much less will we escape if we reject him who warns from heaven. At that time his voice shook the earth, but now he has promised, "Yet once more I will shake not only the earth but also the heavens." This phrase, "Yet once more," indicates the removal of things that are shaken—that is, things that have been made—in order that the things that cannot be shaken may remain. Therefore **let us be grateful for receiving a kingdom that cannot be shaken,** *and thus let us offer to God acceptable worship, with reverence and awe, for our God is a consuming fire.*

— Hebrews 12:25-29

There have been many seasons in my life when I had to surrender my ambitious to-do list for learning to trust God in the middle of my limitations. Whether it was pregnancy, or pneumonia, or our kids' special needs, or just the over-caffeinated ambition of wanting to do it all at Christmas, there have been so many times when I have had to learn (and relearn) that His to-do list is better than mine.

And He really wanted to drill it into me this time, because that baby was due right before Christmas.

That evening, I argued with God (He won, of course) about some things I had been praying for but I didn't trust Him to answer…because, deep inside, I felt like I didn't deserve Him to answer them.

And He reminded me that His answers aren't up to what I deserve.

He reminded me that if I heard a friend say such nonsense, I'd set them straight in a heartbeat.

He asked me why I thought I was so special that His grace applies to others, but not to me.

And He asked me why I felt like I needed to take the credit for His good gifts by earning or deserving them.

Then He asked me to remember this man, my husband, who was unsaved and deeply lost in the beginning of our marriage, but who came to know Him a few years later in such authentic, miraculous ways that I've always known it was only God and not me who did it.

I hadn't even realized I was still carrying legalism and control.

But He asked me if I'd believe His goodness again instead of trusting in my own. And I said yes. Because He always wins – but we do, too, when we surrender.

dark chocolate toffee

Let it be known that it *is* possible to endure four hours of back-to-back dental cleanings for six kids. Let it also be known that if I have to endure such an ordeal, I will celebrate with a sugary latte and two pastries.

On the subject of dental work, did you know that making dark chocolate covered toffee is amazingly easy? Here are my informal directions, and a warning or two. Support your local dentist.

ingredients:
2 cups sugar
1 cup butter
1 cup dark chocolate chips
Magic (Kidding. A sprinkling of coarse sea salt.)

1. Cook butter and sugar together in saucepan on medium high, stirring constantly until it caramelizes (about 8-10 minutes). You'll watch it turn from a pale honey color to deep brown. Tada! This makes toffee! Who knew?!

2. Pour toffee onto Silpat or a parchment paper-lined baking dish, and allow it to cool and harden. Whatever you do, **do not** lick the spoon, no matter how tempted you are to do so, or you will not be able to taste anything for the next three months.
You can make caramel sauce (recipe follows) with all the toffee left in the pot that you can't scrape out.

3 Melt 1 cup dark chocolate in a double boiler. If you don't have a double boiler, fill a saucepan about 1/3 of the way with water and fit a glass bowl inside it so the bottom half of the bowl is submerged in the water while it simmers. Add the chocolate to the bowl and stir gently. Do not over-boil or cook it too fast; the chocolate will seize and you'll have to start over.

4 Spread melted chocolate onto hardened toffee with a rubber spatula.

5 Sprinkle with a little coarse sea salt. (See? Magic!)

6 Refrigerate the whole shebang until hardened, then break into chunks by unceremoniously whacking it on the table or kitchen counter. DO NOT ATTEMPT to karate chop it with your hands. Guess how I know.

7 To save on dentist bills, invite friends over to help you eat it.

P.S. Once, I used apple slices to scrape the pan out with, and then immediately burned my tongue because patience is a virtue I'm still working on. So I suggest making caramel sauce instead, right here:

caramel sauce

1 Pour an ounce or two of heavy cream, milk, or milk substitute into the pot with the remaining toffee that you couldn't scrape from the pot.

2 Turn the heat to medium low and stir, stir, stir…keep going until you work all the toffee into the cream, tipping the pot to the side to work the cream over the hardened toffee on the sides of the pot. Add a little more cream if you need to – the more cream, the runnier the sauce will be.

3 Add it to your coffee, or dip apples in it, or drizzle it over ice cream or your next batch of brownies. You're welcome.

cinnamon french toast dippers

BY MĒGAN ANCHETA

serves 3-4

Kids love finger foods and dipping sauces, which is what inspired this fun recipe. These cinnamon French toast dippers will satisfy the pickiest of eaters and are sure to be a crowd pleaser!

If you are a fan of Dutch Baby Pancakes (puffed pancakes), that's essentially what this recipe is, just a grain-free variation. My girls love it cut into pieces for dipping, but you can serve it however you choose.

Ingredients:
3/4 cup blanched almond flour
1/4 cup arrowroot starch (or tapioca starch)
4 large eggs
3/4 cup almond milk
1/4 teaspoon vanilla extract
1/4 teaspoon ground cinnamon
1 tablespoon coconut oil (for the pan)
maple syrup (for dipping)

1 Place a 12-inch cast iron pan in a cold oven, and preheat the oven to 450 degrees (F).

2 In a blender, combine the blanched almond flour, arrowroot starch, eggs, almond milk and vanilla extract until smooth.

3   When the oven is up to temperature, remove the cast iron pan and brush the inside of it with coconut oil (be very careful as it will be hot). Pour in the batter and sprinkle the top of the batter with cinnamon.

4   Bake for 18-22 minutes, or until a toothpick inserted into the center of the pan comes out clean, and the top is golden brown. Allow it to rest for 5 minutes.

5   Cut the French toast into 1 ½ by 3 ½ inch pieces and serve with a side of pure maple syrup for dipping.

redeemable

I can't tell you how many times in my life I have reached for a pencil behind my ear only to realize I am trying to write with a knitting needle or crochet hook.

I love writing, but I also love all things textile: knitting, quilting, crocheting, embroidery. But one of the main reasons I craft more with yarn than fabric is because yarn is never wasted. Make a mistake? Rip it out, start over, no biggie. But mistakes with fabric are different. You can't mash the mis-cut pieces back together and reroll it like so much clay.

And our days are like fabric, yet He has made us of clay. Our mistakes are never wasted. We are always redeemable. We can't get back our days, and we can't change the past, but God is constantly molding and redeeming us.

At one point in my life I decided I'd never be a mother. At another point in my life, after a traumatic birth followed by a miscarriage a few years later, I thought we might not be able to have more kids.

And at another point seven years later, we had our fourth baby, and with four kids, we thought we were done. Turns out, we were only halfway there. We adopted two more, but we still thought that little girl would always be our youngest.

God proved us wrong twice, in spite of health issues, hormone upheaval, and what was supposed to be fertility-ending surgery. The surgery didn't work, as you know – the doctor said it was his first fail ever – but it was a win for us, twice over.

That doesn't mean it was easy, though.

The surprise pregnancy after that was truly a crisis pregnancy, but it ended up saving our family. It also probably saved my life. And then, the last pregnancy... can I tell you how shocked I was? How I cried for all the wrong reasons when that test said "pregnant," and then cried again when I told my closest friends over the next couple of days? But these two little boys have done me in, tipping the scales toward joy that I never thought was possible before we had them.

I'm grateful to be able to look back now and see what God was doing: Taking the wounded, unlikely, and unqualified, and creating recompense, healing, and abundance. Taking someone who thought she knew who she was and showing how ridiculously off she was from the mark.

That is what God does. **He shows us He knows us** – He knows what we need when we rail against Him and His gifts. We always lose in our striving and grasping for control.

But He brings joy when we trust Him even when it's hard, because we win through surrender. It turns out, our ability to plan and control isn't so important after all. Honoring life is, and the future holds joy for those who do so.

We are a work in progress, and works in progress are often a big mess – like that little Kavanagh, wearing a handknit sweater while standing at the table, eating peanut butter off Finnegan's plate and getting it pretty much everywhere, but I don't care because he's been quiet and happily occupied for about ten minutes. Some days our priorities are just different.

So, these two beautiful boys: two surprises that we never saw coming. We took them to their first candlelight Christmas service, and if there was ever a better picture of God's redemption for us in this beautiful, ridiculous life, I don't know what it is.

We found a knit Christmas vest that Finn only wore once, just in time for Kavanagh to wear it. It had an outline of a reindeer that stretched over his chubby tummy; we *oohed*; we *ahhed*. And then someone said, "Hey, it's Kav's first ugly Christmas sweater!" which sorta ruined the moment.

We found seats at church and sang Silent Night in soft harmony, in tune and off key, while Kav collected all the communion elements, and then hid them in the pockets of the chairs. We found them in time, and Finn insisted on his own piece of communion wafer. But with a look of horrified dismay, he immediately repented when he realized it tasted just like cardboard.

The living warmth of candlelight moved from person to person and row to row, and Finn and Kav, impatiently waiting for excitement, clinked their (unlit) candles together like a toast. As the light was approaching, I watched a little girl a few rows ahead of us wave her candle so close to her father's face that I feared plastic surgery was in his near future.

Trusting a congregation and their children with living fire is such a picture of God's extravagant, reckless faith in us as we handle the gospel and each other with such clumsy hands sometimes.

He knows people might get burned.

He knows we might create a mess.

But He knows that people will see His truth and experience His presence in ways they could not otherwise, without taking those risks. It is the only way to share light until the whole room is glowing — light unstoppable, contagious, driving away darkness, unshrinking, always winning.

He knows it will be beautiful and ridiculous. And He promises — because He is big enough to make it so — that any mess or burning will end up working for our good.

> *And we know that for those who love God all things work together for good, for those who are called according to his purpose.*
> — Romans 8:28

So in that sense, there is no risk, no waste. He has made us clay so we can withstand the heat. He is a good, good Father who delights in teaching his children how to carry His fire.

Now to him who is able
to keep you from stumbling
and to present you *blameless*
before the *presence* of his glory with great *joy*,
to the only God, our Savior,
through Jesus Christ our Lord,
be glory, majesty, dominion, and authority,
before all time and now and forever. Amen.

- jude 24-25

study guide

This flexible, light-yoked guide is for you to use on your own or with a small group. We've included questions to use for personal journaling or group discussion, scripture to study, copy down, and memorize, and short prompts for prayer. It's not homework or another thing to add to your list – it's just movement forward and rest for your soul, friends.

lay it down

questions

What heart issues have I been holding on to that God is asking me to lay down?

What feelings have I been wrestling with that need to be surrendered to God?

What seems far away now? In a year, what might it look like?

scripture

Ephesians 3:14-21

prayer

Lord, help me to hear You so clearly that I am unafraid to move forward in surrender. Tear down the walls I've built up, and show me how trustworthy Your protection is. Thank You for modeling brave love and surrender for me, for my eternal benefit and my present need.

dealing with the mess

questions

What kind of boundaries or rules are currently helping to prevent messes in my life?

Is there a mess that I need to initiate the cleaning on? What should that look like?

In what situation can I choose truth over rumor, gratitude over worry, or grace and forgiveness over hard feelings?

scripture

Zephaniah 3:17, 2 Peter 1:5-8

prayer

Holy Spirit, help me want to clean up my own mess, and to instill boundaries to prevent messes from happening. Give me wisdom and discernment in my relationships and help me forgive those who have made messes I have to deal with. Thank You for knowing my heart, and for rejoicing over my steps of obedience and surrender.

how we thrive when the weather changes

questions

Do I tend to be still to avoid moving? Or do I tend to move to avoid stillness?

Do I currently need to process and find healing in a situation before moving forward?

Who or what have I been tempted to give up on in this season? What might come of that situation if I persist in following God's direction?

scripture

Psalm 105:1-6, 1 Peter 1:13-16

prayer

Jesus, I want to do things Your way. In the places where I am struggling with that, help me to *want* to want Your way. Show me how You are moving and the ways You want to bring healing and joy. Thank You for being the restorer, redeemer, and healer we need.

yielding to His way

questions

What situations in my life cause my emotions to "wrap around the axle?"

Can I identify wrong ways of thinking about these things that contribute to those emotional struggles? How will I tangibly let go and surrender these life situations to the Lord?

Who can I call upon to pray alongside me as I surrender to God's sovereignty in these situations?

scripture

Phillipians 4:6-7, John 14:27, Isaiah 40:28

prayer

Father, I surrender these life situations to you, acknowledging and receiving the peace You give me. Thank you for the peace of Your constant presence and guidance, the peace that surpasses all understanding. I surrender to You, Father, and to Your good plans for my life. Help me to walk courageously into my calling, knowing that nothing takes You by surprise, and that You are always working for my good and Your own glory in and through my life.

made to grow

questions

What is God giving me the opportunity to grow and heal in right now?

How is He nudging me toward alignment and surrender?

Where am I feeling the burn of an uphill climb?

scripture

Philippians 3:12-21

prayer

Jesus, thank You for growing me beyond my mistakes and efforts and failures and second chances. You have made me to succeed in surrender, and to know joy in advancing and moving forward. Help me to cooperate with Your process of healing and growth.

a good plan gone sideways

questions

When have I held on too tightly to my expectations and regretted it? What did I learn from that situation?

What plans do I have coming up soon? How can I hold them loosely?

How can I have realistic expectations while still remaining hope-filled, instead of expecting the worst?

scripture

Romans 8:26-39

prayer

God, help me to see what is true. You hold my days and are in control when unexpected things happen. Thank You for redeeming frustrating situations by using them to mold my character and make me more like You.

surrendered abiding

questions

What have I been resisting or dreading that the Lord is asking me to surrender?

What things is God calling me to fight for, and stand steadfastly in?

What fears am I carrying? What would surrendering those (and walking in freedom without them) look like?

scripture

Jeremiah 37:18—39:4

prayer

Lord, there is such lightness in surrendering the heavy things to You. Help me to release those things quickly, and give me the discernment to know when to fight steadfastly and when to surrender things to You. Your promises are real, for my good, and for the taking, and I choose them over fear from now on.

better than the book

questions

Is there something the Lord has been trying to tell me that I've been ignoring? What am I going to do about that?

When in my life have I surrendered the lesser to embrace the greater that God wanted to give me? How did it refine and encourage me?

scripture

Matthew 14:22-33

prayer

Holy Spirit, You always have my best in mind. You know my heart – where I'm struggling to obey, where I've achieved huge victories, and where I dream of going. Help me to wield surrender well in my life so I can finish well.

overtaken

questions

What have I been praying for that I still don't see yet?

How is God preparing me for it?

How is God asking me to prepare for it?

scripture

Deuteronomy 28

prayer

God, You know my dreams and longings, and You've designed my gifts and talents to be used. I want to prepare well for these longings to be fulfilled, and to cooperate with how You are getting me ready for them. Help me to stay hope-filled and humble before You, and to let go of anything hindering me from the blessings and mission You want to give me.

trading ambition for trust

questions

Where is God stretching me right now? How is it making me more like Him?

How am I doing with observing the Sabbath?

Am I trusting God for the things I cannot do, or am I striving to do everything on my own?

scripture

Jeremiah 17:7-8, Hebrews 12:25-29

prayer

Lord, thank You for trusting me with opportunities to grow and bear fruit. Help me to honor that trust and steward these opportunities well, doing the work I need to do while trusting You with the things that only You can do. Your gifts are so good; I didn't earn them and Your grace is extravagant toward me. I believe in your goodness and know You are doing amazing things beyond what I can see.

redeemable

questions

How has God changed my beliefs about myself or my future?

How has God shown me that He knows me?

How has God trusted me to share light with others?

scripture

1 Thessalonians 5:12-24

prayer

God, You have held my life in your hands so tenderly as You have shaped me, changed me, and drawn me close to You. Help me to be tender with others and myself as I carry Your light. Thank You for trusting me to carry fire, for protecting me from burning, and for redeeming all of my days for Your glory.

1. See John 2:14-15.

2. See Matthew 9:10-12.

3. See Matthew 16:23.

4. Scripture quotation taken from the (NASB®) New American Standard Bible®, Copyright © 1960, 1971, 1977, 1995, 2020 by The Lockman Foundation. Used by permission. All rights reserved. www.lockman.org

5. Marilynne Robinson, *Gilead* (New York: Picador, 2004), 154.

6. Sarah Josepha Hale, taken from "It Snows," 1852.

7. See Jeremiah 37:18-21.

8. See Jeremiah 38:4-6.

9. See Jeremiah 38:8-10.

10. See Jeremiah 38:17-28.

11. See Jeremiah 39:4.

12. C.S. Lewis, *Mere Christianity* (New York: MacMillan Publishing Company, 1952), 94.

13. Ibid, 129.

14. Shannon Guerra, *Oh My Soul* (Wasilla, AK: Copperlight Wood, 2018), 70.

15. Ibid, 70-71.

16. Ibid, 71.

17. See *Abide volume 1: Rest in the Running*, "Upper Room People."

also by shannon guerra

the Work That God Sees series
prayerful motherhood in the midst of the overwhelm

Moms, you pour yourselves out every day. How about some powerful refilling, in small, easy doses?

Short chapters. White space. Deep down hope, and out loud laughter. Because you have what it takes. You are watched over and known by the God who notices every detail, and He meets you in these mundane moments and is breathing them into mighty movement.

Work That God Sees is available as six individual little books, or as a complete, all-in-one edition with the content from all six books (including the snarky recipes, crafty patterns, and questions for personal journaling or small group discussion) plus 25 pages of extra stories, recipes, and lessons you can learn at someone else's expense.

Oh My Soul

encountering God in honest, unconventional (and sometimes messy) prayer

What if there was **one thing** you could do that would always, without fail, make you more **whole** and **healed** and **at peace** than you were the day before...would you do it?

What if, at the same time, that one thing transformed the world around you?

This is what happens when we encounter God, living in His presence, in continual conversation with Him.

We want to hear God better, and to know His will for all the messy, mundane details of our life. But does He still speak to us when we are distracted, grumpy, overwhelmed, and unprepared? How can we have "quiet time" with God when there's no quiet, and no time? Can we really know the will of God and move forward in obedience, in spite of our fears and failures?

And, if we're really honest with Him, will He strike us with lightning? Or will we end up praying with boldness and authenticity like never before?

Available as the original book, companion journal, and 21-day devotional study.

upside down

understanding and supporting attachment in adoptive and foster families

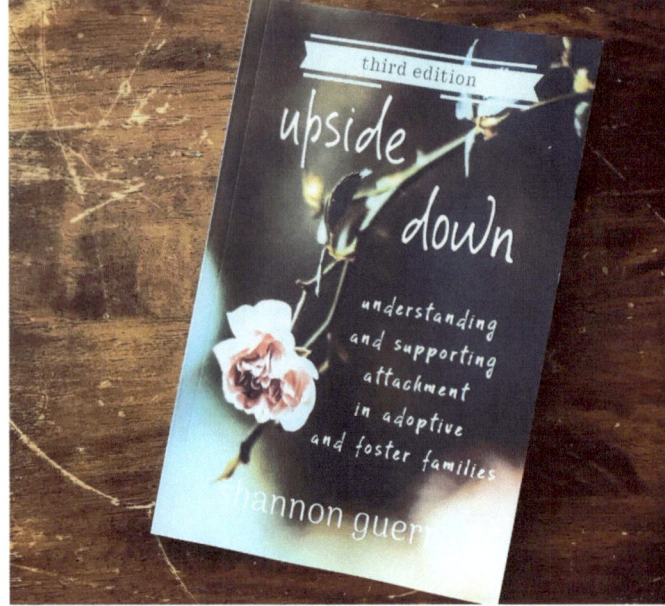

This book gives hope to adoptive and foster families, and the lowdown for those who love them.

Adoptive and foster families working through attachment issues often feel alone, but their communities can intentionally be part of the solution instead of unintentionally being part of the problem. Without that support, adoptive and foster families live in isolation.

Shannon Guerra learned this firsthand after she and her husband adopted two of their children in 2012. She started writing shockingly transparent blog posts about what her family was going through at home, at the doctor's office, and in her heart as a mama.

And then adoptive and foster families started writing back.

Their overwhelming, unanimous theme was, **"This is what I've wanted to tell people for so long. I wish everyone who knows our family could read this."**

This book is the result. In about 100 pages, *Upside Down* provides information and insight that transforms an outsider's assumptions into an insider's powerful perspective. Because adoptive and foster families should never feel alone, and our communities can be equipped to make sure they never feel that way again.

the ABIDE series
a year of growing deep + wide

volume titles:

rest in the running

hope in the waiting

clarity in the longing

bravery for the next step

obedience to move forward

surrendering to win

ABIDE is off the beaten path: A 6-volume series of fully illustrated books that are part devotional, part coffee table book, part magazine. These six beautiful books will lead you further into the presence of God as you grow deep and wide, pressing forward in these seasons that stretch us. Each book contains full color photographs, a light-yoked study section for personal or small group use, an extra recipe or two, and powerful encouragement that meets you where you're at and moves you forward.

one more thing...

Need a little white space in the chaos?

You are warmly invited to copperlightwood.com, where we're transparent about finding peace in the hard moments and beauty in the mess. I hope you'll hit the subscribe button and poke around all the posts and videos. Just keep in mind that it's a little unpolished here, so watch out for the Legos on the floor.

Bless you, friend,
Shannon Guerra

connect:
gab: shannonguerra
mewe: shannonguerra
telegram: Shannon Guerra
clouthub: shannonguerra
goodreads: shannonguerra
pinterest: copperlightwood

email:
shannon@copperlightwood.com

subscribe:
www.copperlightwood.com/subscribe

www.ingramcontent.com/pod-product-compliance
Lightning Source LLC
LaVergne TN
LVHW070259080526
838200LV00067B/469